A Glossary of Snow

A Glossary of Snow

Feral Willcox

Copyright © 2025 Feral Willcox

All rights reserved under International and Pan-American Copyright Conventions. Except for brief quotations in critical articles or reviews, no part of this book may be reproduced in any manner without written permission from the author.

ISBN: 978-1-6653-1042-0 - Paperback
eISBN: 978-1-6653-1043-7 - eBook

These ISBNs are the property of BookLogix for the express purpose of sales and distribution of this title. BookLogix is not responsible for the writing, editing, or design/appearance of this book. The content of this book is the property of the copyright holder only. BookLogix does not hold any ownership of the content of this book and is not liable in any way for the materials contained within. The views and opinions expressed in this book are the property of the Author/Copyright holder, and do not necessarily reflect those of BookLogix.

Cover Art: Feral Willcox

Author Photo: K.L. Graywill

Book Design: Alice Teeter

Printed in the USA

Order online from:
Charis Books & More: www.charisbooksandmore.com or
email info@charisbooksandmore.com

Published by:
Artemis Tales
PO Box 766
Pine Lake, GA 30072-0766

Table of Contents

Introduction	7	sanclist	43
wintalin	11	satin-by-night	44
icinder	12	chelquechine	45
tracewhist	13	aspengown	46
sailshred	14	dove's dress	47
broomlace	15	elban	48
whitavia	16	loscelain	49
starcloth	17	greytread	50
firbone	18	chimerace	51
reticella	19	everliss	52
witchskin	20	daughter of pearl	53
blancmange	21	stillskin	54
hillshroud	22	foxcaste	55
pearlash	23	quistillen	56
breath of Ptarmigan's child	24	quilsprit	57
isselain	25	alcrept	58
mothkinder	26	spiretyne	59
window's cape	27	hillscap	60
owling	28	hillspell	61
stillenta	29	ghost of forest past	62
starswan	30	popeskirt	63
starswan down	31	baker's floor	64
stiltwig	32	elfbeard	65
candace	33	cloudshed	66
ashera	34	Alice's dress	67
queen's grief	35	snow in Scranton	68
bootswallow	36	trilleblanc	69
Lucy's sleep	37	bride of the limb	70
porcelain down	38	canticlere	71
flitesel	39	bride-shed	72
color of pearl	40	celimna	73
starkinder	41		
crysticen	42		
		Publication History	74
		Thanks to	75

Introduction

The book *Landmarks* by Robert Macfarlane came my way at a critical time when I found myself in the international terminal at LAX facing medical and financial exile from the U.S. I had spent the last year camping out in my pickup truck across the country looking for viable options, ending up in Coyote Howls campground in Why, Arizona trying not to wonder just that. My choices in the U.S. after a long period of increasing debilitation were vanishing at an alarming rate. There were no realistic treatments for my disease, and experimental treatments were well beyond my means. My only choice seemed to be a full jump from the paradigms of Western medicine and the strange, limited systems of its practice in my homeland. I sought eastern medicine, then, in the East.

Landmarks is a book about the vanishing language of landscape. The author reclaims an intimacy with the geography of the British Isles by seeking out and restoring a wealth of terminology that has been rapidly eroding. The book was my near constant companion as I entered one of the deepest periods of isolation I'd ever experienced. I was partially housebound with limited mobility in a foreign country where I knew no one and could only hope to find effective treatment for my illness.

Illness, like winter, is a geography of limitation. Both have elements of trance, hypnosis, forced meditation. Both bring a wealth of intimacy brought by a slower pace, a lack of distraction, and by what turned out to be the greatest gift: loneliness. Without these new circumstances, I would have never taken the time to develop this intimacy, the kind that monks meditating in caves would have found, or that average people might have experienced in various seasons during pre-industrial times. A friend posted a video of Kate Bush singing "50 Words for Snow," and my meditative project was born as a love child of her work and Macfarlane's. *A Glossary of Snow* became an extended metaphor for the gifts of illness and isolation and how the limited and particular serve to open whole macrocosmic worlds.

A Glossary of Snow

Feral Willcox

wintalin
> *a greyblue snow that lingers in shadows when other snow has melted*

Snow scraps in shadows stay in places where she wore her lace, between the legs of trees in shadows where she hid her face from rape and tales of rape; frost stays in traces after cancer, whispered rumors of underfeather, tumors where she wore her scraps, a lace of ice tatted to ash in dendritic patterns. This is her body, what's left of see-through winter after cancer, slit womb spills tales of tumors in places snow scraps stay, a lace of rape and tales of rape. This is her body, scattered host in the hollows of rotted frost, rumors of extracted masses chanted at her back as she passes across a tattered damask of cancer, decayed into dendritic lace of rape and tales of rape, shroud of cold earth laid on the body of a girl child at birth.

icinder
> *bright white flakes that dissolve just before they*
> *touch surfaces*

We are lost. Half-lint, half-light, half-life — it is as if a kiss suspends just above the warm lip of every small god begging. But this mistress will not suffer touch; she hovers in near miss and transubstantiates a sacrifice, body of ice, body of ice, to essence: starlight caught in the endless instant of loss.

tracewhist
> *when the snow is sudden and light and leaves a bare hint of an outline on the world, showing the world to be impure*

The tracewist fell, a diagnosis, the land's in a cancer and cannot rest; the dancer turned out of the dance to mud and rubble, cast off post-consumption; the meadow made to lie down for the plow until the tracewist fell, a light cool touch on the exhausted ground, a promise; soon, the long drum, the blanket, and rest; and rest.

sailshred
> *an unexpected snow that comes in sudden gusts,*
> *diverting things from their habitual patterns*

A snow at sea, a storm of sheets in strips,
tongues of snow taste salt, a ship is left to drift,
undriven by wind, and its sandglass spills,

its compass sinks in a sudden thirst, slipping down
below windrose, the surface courses it knows,
its norths and souths, its knots and following sea.

broomlace
> *a coastal snow mixing with spray from the sea*

Near the rocks where the sea witch flies
sprays of lies cold in the snow-blind ways
It's all taxidermy inside where the mafias
of families have eyes engraved with scars
of portraiture. Here is where the bastardies hide
in closets with the brooms of silent wives

whitavia
> *a heavy snow on a dense overstory leaving a hollow,*
> *live silence below*

Something high up watching. The tall tree gods
in their diamond crowns. A clearing at the core,

a distant concern from the realm of the thousand feathered one.
An augury drops down in bones of wing

and their diamond offspring, messages in delicate glyphs.
In shallow snow below, a clearing, a space in the core

of light bones. Listen. In the core of woods, something high up
protects a dim light, sequestered. A tall pine flute;

in its core, a rare breath, a message.
A message in a hint of song from the tall tree gods

and their diamond lore. Something high up spirits lyrics
through the core, messages for us

from the space of nothing, a clearing.

starcloth
> *snow that comes with a dramatic shift in weather*

I'm cold and all I have's a cotton shawl
for a duel with winter; up at dawn, I'm sold
to a day of shiver in the advent of a coming storm.
It's red at night but the color of a cotton shawl
in the east, from whence the weather comes, a duel
between the west and east of color.

Red at night, sailor's delight, but still I'm cold
in a restless wind bound for the rattle of a sill
waking me up at dawn to a coming storm;
a coming storm and all I have's a cotton shawl
against the ills of men and made up makers
in a duel that ends blood red at night.

firbone
> *a permanent snow at high altitudes where
> few survive*

At high altitudes, would she have lived?
If she'd tented herself out, pitched in
with pine scrub growth in its early stages.
If she'd hidden her cages, plucked
her secondary books, would she have loved
and bandaged her pock marked
surge to age, swaddled her pages
diapered her own hearth and home,
would she have burned with the firewood
urges stacked in caskets, would she
have buried her words one two, one two.
If she had lived in arterial surges pumped
one two, secreted in membranes dodging
cold motion, gripped polyps hard married,
clotted in veins. If she had fled
beyond thaw, would she have lived?

reticella
> *snow that falls on screens or grates creating*
> *networks of positive and negative space*

a little net, reticella: a walk through the beginnings of lace
in old magic, in old ice, you will, you are, as in hypnosis

you have, you may, you will cast a spell, senesce, exacerbate
cellular stress in old magic, in old ice. you love roosterman

with a cavalier laugh, madman's apoptotic liesse, stable
arrest where two spots itch, scapular cytoblasts, reticence
where wings were, will be

caduceus to bone lace wilderness. how to cook a butterfly,
how to send a spotted lanternfly into trance, in old magic,
in old ice

witchskin
> *a snow that outlines the limbs and branches of deciduous trees in winter*

In a land of white white sin, a cold so deep it stops water and cold milk in a frozen mother. When we speak of witches' tits, that kind of cold, with remembered skin on coals of limbs. She's a witch who sinks or swims, breathes out or in when a flame wavers or stays true to still life etched in ice. She's a witch who bobs up once, or twice, screams three times or is silent as snow and cold when she's tested again at the end.

In a land of white white men, a silver scene etched out of tin and tested against machine-made lace in linen trim. She's a witch who marries or doesn't marry him.

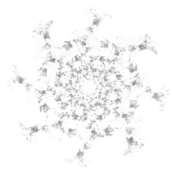

blancmange
> *when an icing of snow turns the world to*
> *a confection*

The snow fell sweet, parfait, blancmange, pale on spirit of pale
Three children seen through isinglass, a crumb, a smear, a blur
She said I need my stars to sleep, pale on spirit of ground

She said, I need sleep, dark and sweet, night gone stale
marron glace draped in veils of light, scarves, skirts whirl
a world to luminesce, pale on spirit of pale

Three children phosphoresce, lost, as winds turn tail
in cotton candy streets. The mutt, the growl, the cur
Where light falls grated from the moon,
      pale on spirit of ground

We are lost in ossuaries, interred in milk sweet layers of shale
She said, it's trickery, fracked to quake, electric saboteur
We are lost in roots of deciduous teeth, pale on spirit of pale

I need my stars to sleep, she said, her cerements swept into sail
Three children, trapped in gelatin fluoresce, a wisp, a swipe, a slur
a sugared creep, circadian, pale on spirit of ground

From a pastried mania of light, storms unveil
the left-behinds, forgot-abouts,
      dropped from a streaming pace incur
a peace of night, three children found outside the jail,
      pale on spirit of pale
She said, I need my stars to sleep, pale on spirit of ground

hillshroud
> *the friendly surroundings disappear in snow when*
> *the sky is white*

She disappeared. White into white, dark from dark. Hitched up her petticoats in fists and booted off post-haste into Les Cloches de Saint-Exupéry. The diamond died, quiet in the mine. I tried to find her, but there was no shine; the horizon hid between bride/not-bride. I knew she loved that line.

pearlash
> *a late snow that alternately melts and rises*

a dust of pearlash, a dandruff
on my cathemeral world; a harebell ghost
rings in soft silence at the neck of the rock
where I choke back smoke
Fall, flakes, fall into my open mouth
leavened sounds soft as risen cakes
even now, sing me down

breath of Ptarmigan's child
> *a scant snow atop a deeper snow adding a light
> motion at the surface*

Shadow of a shed feather
snowprint of a twig's spirit
whiteshade drift of a minute
beak black speck in a blizzard of acres
the tundra turns in a nestling's breath
a vast and instant shift

isselain
> *snow falling in shifting and near transparent sheets,*
> *providing hidden parallels of time*

Reindeer swim in a carved bone tale
seek reprieve in narrows of worlds
Between veils scrolled with spills of pearls
frail as peals of cold bells, storied orbs
collide with probability clouds, incite
carved ivories of brides to flight

mothkinder
> *a snow with winged flakes that seem to move up and down in the air without ever falling*

In the underdream of another time,
a gyroscopic scandal of math, slant of a tangent

twirled in drift minus draft, planet-tilt-a-whirl
gimbaled by fickle forces. How many flakes

will make it to land? The warming gamble is on.
The flakes fall up in a lottery puff; they won't

come to rest. No winner declared, none to be found.
Even the house is sleeping now.

window's cape
> *a steady, deep snow, blowing in from a single*
> *direction for days on end, making snow horizons on*
> *each windowpane*

In window's cape, all are solitary now, and slow; no plow
for it, no sled or sleigh or shoe, nothing to do but stay.

The mind, an organ, warmed into visions, trapped in fits
of distraction, winter sweats, paces, rages, chunks of peat hurled

at hearth, 'til the body calms and the tethered head comes in
from the storm, then eons of silence until firesong surrounds
the cauldron,

sings in the seaweed soups of the cold islands, clearing the blood
of its racing and dust, the heart of its rust, Mary at the foot, Brigid

at the head 'til the coming of the day, the coming of days and days
of this, nothing but this.

owling
> *a thick, seemingly fibrous snow, falling from thick,*
> *seemingly fibrous clouds*

who's chosen? pick of the dozen
moved from ovens of bones
to plant brooms in the commons
who smuggles wool from the bottoms?

the role of the cloven, to know
what's stolen, pick of the coven
sold off the land to towns
by crowned ones
of the owned world

now she knocks on your door
peddling doves and hosen,
woolens, gloves, poison
whose hooves are those? riven
prints as skirts sweep snow
and mavens go

stillenta
> *a snow that blows in on a relentless,
> mechanical wind*

The wind is cold. The ground is cold. And in the trees, a sovereignty. Who rules the snow? Who knows its ways? The motive, cold. The profit, cold. And in the trees, the starlings dream. The song is cold. The ground is cold. The motive, cold, can lead to colder days. Who knows its ways?

The song is cold, and singing froze. In freezing air, the starlings dream. To colder days and colder seas, cold machines can lead the way. In freezing air we tried our song. The night grew long, and singing froze. Cold machines, in colder rooms made frozen dreams and colder seas.

The night grew long, and froze the days; the motive, still. We tried our song, made frozen dreams from colder ways. The cold ones chose in colder rooms. The motive, still. The profit, cold. Who rules the snow, and froze the days? The cold ones chose a sovereignty.

The wind is cold, from colder ways.

starswan
> *an elegant snow that seems to float in from a high white sky, rather than falling clumsily from blubbery clouds*

A distant charity descends, a ball, white on white; hints of laughter echo, faint clinks of glass, holograms of long elegant necks, fluffed buttresses, puffs of nothings, whims, meringues, insubstantial whiffs of things, vapors of waiters with swirling trays serving distillations of essences, impressions, reputations.

They are ghosts of themselves, scenes behind scrims, translucent as memories in solutions of gin, lacking nothing, they thin, silken in the winter wind, particles waving by in white-on-white floats pivoting spirits of gloves, they descend.

starswan down
> *an irregular snow, drifting high in places, while leaving no trace in others*

The Earl of Grey has lost his tea, his valet and his kitchen maid. Now he wanders the grounds in his stockings leaving white footprints, and powdered spots of wigshed from his do, askew on his wobbling head. He carries the tea-seeking cream, carelessly hooked to a long curled finger, drips out dollops randomly in zigzags, starswan down. Now and again he takes a tea-less sip, then sprays it out in a stipple.

He is not unhappy with his lot. He knows he will soon come across the fox, and the dogs will run, and yelp, run and yelp and run.

stiltwig
> *a snow that, once fallen, holds it shape for a short time*

Can you see me beneath my fine hat?
It is ten times as tall as me.
I hoped that you would notice
and not think me ordinary.
I hoped that you would not think of me at all,
but only of my fine hat, piled high, piled high
upon my ordinary head.

If you knew the truth,
the truth of me, you'd see
I was in a shivering skin,
and you might not buy my white blankets,
my snow white trinkets, illusions I vend
to perpetuate the vacuous wealth of my hat,
my fine hat, piled high, piled high
upon my ordinary head.

candace
> *a snow ruled by wind, entirely governed in its*
> *nature by patterns of wind*

Dear England in winter, where are your bears? I'm drunk on the flight of your snowy owls, and I cannot find Iceland anywhere. An island's wings disappear in salt and frost. Am I flying again? High on the air of stirring storms. Dear England, why did you send me so far from home,

in search of your bears; your kings and queens, their heirs, promising pillows of snow in the air. If only a forest grew here. I'm drunk on sea froth coughed up into scares of snow; winds from the Isles of Eyre whirl below. I'm flying again to the nowhere home. Dear England, where are your bears?

ashera
> *a dissociated snow, falling unnoticed on abandoned land*

A year of astronomers startled
the eye of Sauron - a distant
swirling doughnut of doom
falling in light ribbons
back to an eye, a nested
method to pry more secrets from the maw
of science demonstrating the rings
of globe-girding resolutions
We're carved into a day like veins
through fields of drifting cashiers, lightly
tethered in the dying galaxies of malls
Scatter them gently with their constellations
of sales falling in flakes
to the frozen pale
The eye of capital
moves on

queen's grief
> *a sudden, unexpected snow covered quickly with a thin polish of ice*

In the time of fine china and pearl, enamel thin
and brittle, yet strong as stone and etched
in bone-real braille, not sadness, but an edict of it,
witnessed and sealed, and the young sent off stalking
with the Royal Consort at Balmoral; the queen's grief
swiftly and silently fell.

bootswallow
> *thick heavy snow deep as deer knees*

The real crone, you don't know. She'll speak
for a shekel through any old crow, a glottal caw
of a heckle when you're stuck out back
of a brickyard barn in a bootswallow snow
that turns swans to stone, flesh to bone; ten to one
there's a crick in your neck from looking back
at a peck of a glimmer, the baked-on con of a winner.

Don't truck with the slack-jawed clone droning on
from a neck-tied throttle — she is not your mother.
The real crone may joke, but she's got the track in her scope.

She always speaks in three's, your choices: follow the love,
follow the money, follow the love of money.

Lucy's sleep
> *a season of snow that marks a shift from one era
> to another*

Clouds in habits clothe over
the half-dry child, once limber in winter,
now still as a log capsized. Take the clothes
off of love; build a fire. The body slowly dries.
Silence listens to older ones, gold leaves
rotted in piles, apples half-blackened;
exhausted guillotine eyes shut very suddenly
by sleep slice off something of thinking
into beer fluff piles. Finally she cries,
rinsing away imperial times.

porcelain down
> *a sheet of snow covering a flat field once used for sport or battle*

The field is done with the sport of war, has given up the ghost of grid, released from cults of more and territory, turf spar and parry, combustion fast, falling blast, drone borne bomb to quarry, all now buried here.

It was the soldier, at last, who stopped it one day. Just walked away, gathered up the flags, the undone drums, explosions, applause, orgasms of cheers, of force and torture. His eyes, he knew, would never again see as they did when he was young; but his child, he swore, would never set foot on this field, now covered with porcelain down

the thin and brittle sheet of grief that always falls on the corpse of more, wherever it dies, from sport or war.

flitesel
> *snow that blows in when the door is opened*

How dark it was, not so long ago.
By the light of evil eyes, snow fell
from the skies. When the moon was new,
no one knew what came in, by the way
of doors. Perhaps it was the paper poor,
confetti thin, who blew in. And the questions
asked by tails of voles, curled around the world,
answered when the moon was full,
even then, we'd not see everything that blew in,
by the way of opened doors.

color of pearl
> *a tainted snow, the color of pearl*

The mother of the color of pearl. The dull color
of mother. The smooth cover. The egg shell.
The cotton wool. Red rover red rover send sylvia over.

The partial color. The color of dove, but unwinged,
ring necked, scarved. The color of strangle, wrangle,
love. The oven. The buns in it. The color of clover.

The perfect mother. The pearl. The color of dun.
The debt collector. The swift remittance. The glove.
The winged left-over. Hand flapping, done.

The tomb cover. The driver. The mother of stoves,
of hot cross-over. The sun gone down. The well,
the ping of it coined. The soil, the return, the stone.

starkinder
> *a crystalline snow that can trick the innocent*

An ice creeps in to eyesight,
fractures cataracts across the glass.
An illusion of diamonds comes
from light in the eyes of children,

and fractures cataracts across the glass
refracting fire from its place,
from light in the eyes of children
through the foxes' paths

refracting fire from its place
into the bone-white landscape
through the foxes' paths
as he's collecting matches

from the bone-white landscape of facts.
An illusion of diamonds comes
as he's collecting matches
and ice creeps in to eyesight.

crysticen
> *snow that covers melting ice, breaking apart on a lake*

See her, under ice, her drink, sea-glass
green, lost chalice of ice, porcelain clink
of glass on sink. See her think in teacup
chime, spilling iridescent iris

green, lost chalice in a purse clinks
metallic, kissing ice, her drink now twice
chimed, spilling palace in an iris
tempest, cursed. See her think the past

metallic, kissing friends, now lost twice,
poem crumpled in a purse, cursive
tempest, cursed. The ice, too thick, the past,
a fantasy, a palace in a glass.

A poem, crumpled in the trash, cursive
evidence, a friend, now lost, immersed
in fantasy, her story etched in glass.
See her under ice, too thick, coerced

by evidence of silver past, immersed
at last in verse, in the trash of breaking,
reach her under frozen spell, coerced,
once, now twice from story etched in wish.

At last, in verse, iridescent, breaking
glass on sink of silver past, teacup,
once, now twice, iced porcelain of wish
to see her under frozen spell of glass.

sanclist
> *a snow that creates cave-like spaces where all
> manner of creatures hide through freezing times.*

Cold, and the child, semi-wild, old
and the window piled high,
tide and the night shade, liquor held tight
while a child in the light smiled and sold
herself again

for a sample of wrinkled skin
turned in, her secret burned
on the back of her seeking, sin
and the fold of god, all told but no
telling of when

she gets out again

Come here under the blanket
and I will tell you what they did:
They skewered her with god
and scraped off her skin
Thus was she groomed to smile
in a fevered code of sucked up love
sex shriveled small
in a hidden skein of lies

Here is a song for her. Here is a song
for the pagan child, three stories old, lost
in the lore of lords, rolled up tomes of soldiers
scrolled over the sounding fables of her and her kind

From the common book of fires:
Something's burning in the kitchen; and again
she smiles, liquid gold underthings owned
and bone dense waiting blooms
to glass. A sullen slavery names her,
but all wild by night and then

satin-by-night
  snow on the surface of a frozen lake

The ice at the surface is far, so far, from the boiling core, the boiling core that warms the dreams of sleeping fish, the boiling core that warms the songs in their minds as they lie dormant, as they lie still and sunk against the rocks and crags of the cold lake floor, as they lie

still in the strata of cold and colder water, the strata of an archaeology of lies, repeated in sedimentary stages until they harden in the cold throughout the cold and colder ages.

The skater at the surface is perpetual in her motion. In her motion, she etches her words in the snow on the surface of a frozen lake, making scraps of the satin snow, she etches her words with the blades of her skates in the satin snow on the surface: This is what happened here. This is what happened to me.

Maybe the snow covers over what she wrote before, maybe the snow covers over her perpetual work. Maybe the wind blows away her words. Maybe she doesn't care.

The story she traces will be ignored, retold in cold and colder lies, frozen smiles and pies: everything's fine. But still she skates night after night, retelling in lines traced on the ice of cold and colder times, frozen smiles and pies, night after night: Everything's fine.

But a culture is formed by its lies. Perpetually she skates, with focus and devotion, propelled by an essence of emotion: This is what happened here. This is what happened to me. So far from the boiling core.

chelquechine
    a bright snow against day-blue sky

After it happens,
some never speak again,
some never smile,
and some
come upon a day
that cracks open the vaults of blues,
peals of bright skies,
loud bright blues
almost like sounds,
something like bells,
and they cry.

aspengown
> *the forested mountains, dressed in snow, dance with
> the moon*

I have your moon. It rose up over snow as the last rose glow went to mist behind the mountain. I caught it with my bow, arrowed in and reeled it to my side. I have your moon, captive in my mind.

I held your snow. I froze my hand to keep it cold. It made a white hand of mine, and tempted as I was to drop or throw, I chose this glove, and even in my sleep, I held your snow.

I kept your peace. Sweet as forest breeze in fir, a secret peace of trees, I kept the spirit of this place bathed in birdsong even when the birds were gone, even when there were no trees, I kept your peace.

I have your moon, your snow, your peace, soaked into my bones, and when they bury me, all will be released.

dove's dress
>   *snow that sings as it flies*

Remember this: a broom's wish, best, a song
unsettled from a startled nest, the underskirt of lyric white
sings to offspring left in twig and ice, dove's dress
fluttered in sudden draft lifts in flight from the crest
of feathered breath. Remember this:
your mother left in fright
singing secrets of regret.

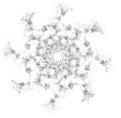

elban
> *clumps of snow dropping from a laden surface*

a bubble, a vesicle, a bulla
arranged by their strangeness
snow clods, thuds, pom, pom
timpanic, resonant,

and of the laden mother
pom, pom, a bleb, a bubble
of one mineral within another

timpanic, resonant,
so that total strangeness is conserved
bound by an algorithm of calvin
which allows total strangeness to change

the second generation of matter
here are the polymers that justify her
and other charmed particles

when subtracted from total charm
Listen: skry the duds of snow, pom
pom, where's home?

    Note: "Pom pom" is borrowed from Sylvia Plath "The Swarm"

loscelain
> *a hardened snow that does not reveal its secrets*

Oh holy night, another cold layer of her on the phone, cold
layer of snow, and her voice clear:
>   You're an artist, disappear

as I always did, covered over in her daily snows, my holy
nights of carnal sweet, lost in sheets,
stolen archives of my days cataloged in layers of her brittle
tales of frozen over hells fixed in fear
that even one real smile would bring a thaw, send demons
running for rum, frozen sins exposed, dripping in the sun.

Now stars are brightly shining, here in another cold New Year,
motherless now but for the habit, to conceal, with each new
snow, anything that might have shown my life to be my own.
How to reverse my art, spell to curse, curse to spell;
>   how to reappear?

how to extract myself from the bible of her snows, pages
crystalline and sharp, but fragile, and she, always begging
us not to leave her alone in the cold immobile religion of her
world. We broke her every time we smiled.

greytread
> *a degraded snow, collected by the sides of roads*

Running out of candles, losing bees, dropping like flies losing flight, eyes losing bright, the bathmat dries, losing drops of tears to skies, running out of lamp wicks and oil, low on totems, oranges, no more, nor friends nearby, and families fight tearing trust from the barest cloth between skin and cold wind, all holy gone from night.

I am song hungry, lack drunk, and sick with box-boomed sound, thin electric tunes tubed and twittered through the ether world, lobbed into ear spirals, tickling cochlea but no gut string plucked, twanging blood rush up to chest, frozen mid-breath, a music motionless as death.

If this season has warmth, it's elsewhere, in some European remnant of quaint puddings and plums. Here, I'm warming to a memory of belonging, the heat of it long gone.

chimerace
> *a hypnotic snow that draws a stare, then a vision*
> *or hallucination*

On the harsh path pulled along as if in a belled sleigh behind
a troika of unbridled mares, freezing nostrils, steaming haunches,

into a blizzard barred with birch, we flinch at low branches.
It takes years to remember true kindness. Novices lash

at their own flesh with their justices, leap out at us from brush
in flares of judgements - they'd be dragons in another age. Now

they inhabit the most innocuous places, serving tea in the corners
of visions, offering cakes of hallucinations. She is my only
      love, and yet

the mares pull me away. She is screaming as I go. She says if I leave,
I will always be cold. The mares pull me deeper into snow.

everliss
> *snow that falls in places where there is always snow*

What seems vast
is encased, in it we float, everlost
in a snow-globe home, cold glass
scope, molten dome frozen
over us, skewered
on a brittle steeple of trust —
it would always be like this, everliss:
snow, home grown,
what we've always known.
To get away from her,
how far we'd go,
cold mother of snow,
the predestined church
that follows us.

daughter of pearl
> *a hard snow born from a harder snow, under the*
> *hard shell of a dull grey sky*

In an era of hollow dolls lost in warspell, sororities of the pearled-up poor, glamour girls pushed from great depressions into chorus lines, high kicks and cattle calls of drunken flesh swirled in a syrupy cocktail of dresses, pleats and flounces, cleavages, pearlescent romances, crooning juniors of blue-blood seniors, shills of swindlers, big brass boards of hidden hitlers melting their silver spoons into shrapnel kisses milked from winter skies uddered with promises, falling, falling as tin cups fill with snow and rattle off into the steaming rubble of true love, I'll be waiting for you, dear, with home appliances and recipes, the basics of home-economics: the rich give a gift to the poor, another war.

Girls born from girls born from girls, daughter of pearl, a hard snow born from a harder snow, under the hard shell of a dull grey sky.

stillskin
> *a snow so dry and fine that it perfectly traces the surfaces on which it falls*

In a snow so dry and fine, the flake, unique, released from the moist pull of its sisters, can then perceive the crevice or ridge of a print, whorls, islands of a finger of grass or carcass, nothing like it in the world, the hair of a wrist, a miracle, and here a trace of the coast of atlantis, or a reflection of the forests of mars, raised in bas relief on dying leaf, erased but for the memory of this silken skin, still as the ache of the traveler returned, leaning on a familiar door. Please say you remember me.

foxcaste
> *when snow finally claims the landscape as its own*

The taiga recedes; calligraphies of trees bleed out to a vast flat peace of snow. Tyrants reincarnate here, stake their fantastic claims. In summer, they'll briefly own some lichen, their new subjects immune to coercion, alpine fox or hare, chimeras of shamans with drums.

In winter they are drenched in stark lack, forced to notice breath, cold in their chests. There is no one to hear them in their new realms. They listen now.

There are those who would say they own the land. No one can own the land.

quistillen
> *a snow combined with sleet that makes a ringing sound as it falls*

The silence, when it comes, terrifies the mind, a silence of snow falling on snow falling on snow. But we are not cold. From this silence comes the sleetsnow notes, tuning quistillen to tines of iced twigs and spokes of fir spray chimes, a moment's notice that underneath the roar of things, everything sings.

quilsprit
> *a tiny particulate sleet-snow that pierces and stings*

> Did it come like an arrow, did it come like a knife?
> Sylvia Plath, from 'The Detective'

Did it come like ants to a party? Shrapnel
to a body? Chisels to crystal? Did it come like
a garden? a cancer? a warning?

Was it more like peace, or more like war,
the storm? That sliced sky and turned
high laughs to glass. We were thrice

removed from the blast. Once, we danced,
twice we prayed, then we wept. What fell?
Snow or ash? Did it come well dressed?

With child? Enriched? We took the bit,
bought the gas. Ignored the forecast:
Winter to a warming.

alcrept
> *long days and nights of a tiny particulate snow*
> *falling on dry drifts and influenced by a hint of*
> *wind, light, but steady, until the landscape is*
> *entirely changed without any noticeable event*

From the flicker and stutter of indoor power, all outside
appears a grey aquarium as alcrept comes, tint click specks

at glass, crustacean ticks on seafloor, quilts of scripture unsutured
into scraps and patches, now adrift in endless waves of zikr

old as sturgeon, listed tenets of religion, liturgies of fishes form
and unform in requiems of themselves, as grey layered currents

shift whole histories in minutes. Then let the activist rest,
as the delicate drift persists, unlit, undriven

When we wake, in a fortnight, all will be changed, and no shot fired,
no severed heads, no one jailed, no congress entrained.

spiretyne
> *a snow that hugs the sides of vertical things*

Sheets of moths fall blanched and stunned in a wind,
forget what they know of wings, move in a longing whine
towards moonshine on the sides of things, walls, trunks,
spires, inclines of all kinds while the moon herself eludes
any clamber or climb and whole choirs of us fall silent
from a striving height, saved at last from our old habit
of digging with spoons in a lunar mine for light.

hillscap
> *the second snow of the season, falling only at*
> *altitude without impact in the valley towns*

It is snow in a scapular patch, neatly flipped up on the mountain's top, a scrap of storm sewn into a quilted landscape, domesticated weather as it decorates the mayor's foyer, picture perfect, measuring just a few inches more than the year before.

hillspell
> *when the surrounding land still shows itself, but*
> *begins to give away its identity to the snow*

Now you see me, now I fade, last scraps
of color, volition, choice, fall from sleeping trees;
hillspell wands away all all sun and summer;
all evidence of me dissipates, quiets.

Now you see me, now I spin,
gowns of waltzing thought slough off
in dervish whirl to stillspin, mind en pointe,
turning, turning. Now you see me, now I fall boneless
into caveshell, surrender to effortless rest, dream
a fern of a new spine unfurling.

ghost of forest past
> *a snow that seems to fall on unseen shapes, evoking*
> *a landscape that no longer exists*

When once she was wild with tree and unwrapped
from glass, snow fell upon her in a tryst, and she glistened then
with lust, with frosted tips of fir and birch. Now
the snow-made groves disperse in a concrete curse; now alone,
the snow remembers her.

popeskirt
> *a snow that accumulates in flame-like peaks*

A fire in heaven gone wild, spills
molten gold down to lower realms as snows fall
in frozen-over hells; heavenly choirs spill down
on rivers of molten golden bells; falling angels
cool in tell-all rills far from the sun god's favor.

Cooling hells fill with melting gates
of pearl, in the swill of tell-all tales,
testaments, protection rackets cracking
popeskirts into silver bells.

Freed from the heat of the war god's fury,
trips of risen devils scatter up alps
through talus and scree, loosened choss
of rotten rock. The mobster gods
have forgotten us.

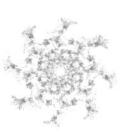

baker's floor
> *a dusting of snow, a light powder, that swirls up in the wind*

A sudden whiff of soup, chicken lentil
and mystery, gusts up a day's story from
the baker's floor, infiltrates cracks
in the flatbread of mastery, spins a myth
to ignite the white math of wind.

elfbeard
> *a snow that prefers hollows and cavernous aspects of land, seeming to avoid open spaces*

We who are small live longer, and our whiskers and buns increase for centuries like the trees in whose shadows we hide 'til the hair of both genders is longer even than we who are small and hiding in places you cannot or do not see.

You who are tall live much shorter, and shorn are your faces, cropped are your curls, bare is the land you inhabit, exposed as you are with your guns and your swords, wild pistons loosed from their engines reigning like gods in your skies,

while we who are small simply hide in the places you cannot or do not see; the meek who'll inherit are we.

cloudshed
> *a heavy snow that comes when a geographic feature causes all the precipitation to drop out of a system at once, making a qualitative distinction between one side of the feature and the other*

She is holy with desire, swollen with storm and strong from so many treks and exiles, to get up next to that mountain, ink black in the dusk, on one side dry and heartless, on the other begging for the snow of her, veined with creek beds, waiting. And could cloudshed wrench the entire avalanche from a system laden with the rains of all londons, all monsoons, held-back tears from unwanted touches of five thousand years?

The day rape ended, the snowmelt came, the plains flooded, the wetlands filled with joy, and the sea changed five thousand times.

Alice's dress
> *a snow that is delicate and fine as subtle thought*
> *forms, intuitions*

What is it about the feather, white as sky, drifting
across an ice-clad river to rest just here, in the snowprint
of a lost sister, her head dressed in wild lace and grey
formed thoughts, an overlay of fine thin snow

on the rugged concepts of commerce and physics, a prayer
where there would be only high drifts against towers
of academics. But hers is a prayer of fashion, evidenced
in the subtlest embroidery of pink flush on the disappearing

arctic at sunset, a prayer of tundra for her lace, her dress,
    her blush.

snow in Scranton
> *a mercurial snow that blows from one direction, then another, and changes in quality from one minute to the next*

Back then, when the snow came in with a shifting wind, you were the boygirl bird, flown in with your curls from the renaissance of England, and I was something with fur, coming in from the virgin wood of the new world; how far we sailed in the teacup ship as whole dimensions sprang up from table-top maps, as the habitual fortunes of stars broke out from sanskrit into wild line drawings, tree branches releasing the etchings of industry from a coal grey sky.

Back then, before I knew how longing hid in a painting of cranberries and pears dripping from trees reflected in window grids tipped with frost, and how flames blazing in stacks of brick could warm up a hunger of angels screaming for nothing but the sound of you, the sound of you laughing; back then the light was always changing.

You don't always know what I am feeling, basking in a slew of invitations, hectic strings of thirsty friends — one wants whiskey, one wants coffee, one wants some insipid herbal tea. When I left you, you were still breathing, but your lips were blue with school, songs dissolving on the floor around you leaked from plastic caskets opened for grace, after a party. I have been sealed off, you said, and then you disappeared again, leaving me leaning with my back against a well, wanting water

then singing for the rest of my years of a single mercurial tear that made into a tiny bell, ringing once before it fell. Now someone I love enters the room, asking, finally, if I need a lullaby, or a blanket as the snow blows in steady from the north-northwest, and the cold weather is holding.

after a poem by Frank O'Hara

trilleblanc
> *a warm, wet snow, falling in flower-sized flakes*

Sky gardens, winter's trillium,
falling petals trace out descending smiles,
drift up, slip down, drift up; night blooms
into blankets for a dreaming land.

A widow sleeps, her hair
undone; her hand drops
down touches root-borne visions
come unbound.

bride of the limb
> *when the snow is heavy and wet and married to surfaces*

If you are in the way of such a snow, she will love you: the broken branch, the plastic trash, every aspect of coal and ash, touched. And if you are birch or lonely post, you're taken off to church with all the world in the way of such a snow. If you were unknown in the wood, a mere trellis of such unthunder as passed for a scratch, a hint of distraction in a patch of grass, prepare to be wed by the bride of the limb. All known, all chosen in snow.

canticlere
> *a snow that has already fallen, remaining still in
> cold air after the storm has passed*

When joy is silver, in the light of a high thin moon,
frozen spells of bellchoirs, cold peals of aeolian chimes
echo across a frozen lake,

a lone cantor chants harmonic minor, descant cast
in an ice-blue gleam; when joy is silver and alone,
spirit of a loon in the hollow of a flute, a silver truth

stark in the deep of night, and no one to die with, a private joy,
a rare visitor before it comes to stay.

bride-shed
> *a pearlescent snow draped over shallow hills that seems to glow from within in a slight melt from a bright sun*

The sky undresses.

celimna
> *a snow that enhances understanding of the*
> *underlying forms of objects by obscuring most*
> *of their presenting qualities to reveal their most*
> *essential natures*

In the dark hour that sweeps over
the sleeping world, when nuns rise up
to chant the language of flower ghosts;
chalk petals, pearls of cold dew, stamens
on tongues conjure new stems
in a celibate light to mate tendrils
of song with lost meaning.

Celimna, sung down from sutras
adrift in the storm, rings into form
the flower's essence: a question:

What do you want?
Yes, you, there, on your knees.
What do you want?

Publication History

Per Contra. Issue 37

Glossary of Snow	tracewhist
Glossary of Snow	bride of the limb
Glossary of Snow	dove's dress
Glossary of Snow	ghost of forest past
Glossary of Snow	hillshroud
Glossary of Snow	baker's floor
Glossary of Snow	queen's grief
Glossary of Snow	porcelain down
Glossary of Snow	breath of Ptarmigan's child
Glossary of Snow	trilleblanc
Glossary of Snow	icinder
Glossary of Snow	crysticen, published as "Lost Friend"
Glossary of Snow	aspengown, published as "I have your moon"

Peacock Journal, January 18, 2017

Glossary of Snow	Alice's dress
Glossary of Snow	starswan
Glossary of Snow	celimna
Glossary of Snow	sailshred
Glossary of Snow	canticlere

Plath Poetry Project

        snow in Scranton

(This poem, after Frank O'Hara, contains his lines "You don't always know what I am feeling" and "For Grace, after a party")

Rogue Agent. Issue 49

        wintalin

About Place

        alcrept

The Mackinaw

        daughter of pearl

Thanks to...

All the lifelong mentors from writer's groups, for these poems especially Chiang Mai poets Rosalie Wilmot, Sara Luisa, Rebecca Weldon, Mark Rossiter, Richard Oyama, Heather Joy Gatley, Lorri and Geoffrey Pimlott, Sybil Turnbull, Sandra Wright, Ina Solum, Polly Szantor, and stateside Alice Teeter, Meredith Rose, Debra Hiers, Amanda Gable, Kay Hagan, Celeste Tibbets, Melissa Tidwell, Leslie Williams, Kathleen Culver, Susan Marynowski, Aliesa Zoecklein, Samara Powers, Michele Sharp, Joan Larkin, Victoria Boynton, Jessica Logreira, Yadi Flannery, Bear Sahlfeld, Pat Guerard, Andria Olinger, all the women in the amazing Truth or Consequences Women's writer's group, editorial and other help from John Sibley Williams, Elaine McCarthy, Kathie deNobriga, Melanie Almeder, Laurie Cubbin, Randi Cameon, Warren Muller, Michael Biello, Dan Martin, Lou Pesce, Doug Willcox, David and Pam Willcox and family.

www.ingramcontent.com/pod-product-compliance
Lightning Source LLC
Chambersburg PA
CBHW072139070526
44585CB00016B/1743